WILD RIVERS

WILD RIVERS was first published in the last months of the campaign
to save Tasmania's wild rivers from the Gordon-below-Franklin dam.
The text was completed as the bulldozers moved towards the wilderness.
Events in the campaign continued to move swiftly.
In the spring of 1982 there were large "No Dams" rallies in mainland cities.
But on December 8th, Prime Minister Fraser's government dismayed many
Australians by declaring its support for the dam.

On December 14th, a meeting of UNESCO in Paris proclaimed the Tasmanian
wilderness a "World Heritage" region. On the same day, in the rainforests
beside the Gordon and Franklin Rivers, a peaceful blockade of the
dam works began. In the ensuing weeks 1,500 of the 6,000 people who
were part of the blockade effort were arrested. Hundreds were jailed.
These events gained worldwide headlines.

On February 4th, 1983, nearly 20,000 people jammed the streets of
Tasmania's capital, Hobart, in the largest land conservation rally
in Australian history. One day earlier, a national election had been called.
Conservationists launched a massive campaign.
On March 5th Mr Fraser's government fell. The new Prime Minister, Mr Hawke,
pledged to stop the dam. Citing Australia's World Heritage Convention
obligations, his government took the case to the High Court.
A long legal battle ensued.

At 10.40 a.m. on July 1st, 1983, the High Court of Australia declared the
dam works illegal. By early September, the last of the Hydro-Electric
Commission's machinery was withdrawn from the wilderness.
The wild rivers were left to run free to the sea.

The book has become a celebration of a heartfelt community effort
which succeeded; and of a beautiful part of the original Earth
which has therefore survived.

FRANKLIN/DENISON/GORDON
WILD RIVERS

photographs by Peter Dombrovskis
text by Bob Brown

for Olegas Truchanas

PUBLISHED & DISTRIBUTED BY PETER DOMBROVSKIS PTY LTD
P.O. Box 245, Sandy Bay, Tasmania 7005 Australia

First Published June, 1983
Second edition published December, 1983

National Library of Australia Card Number and ISBN 0 9597530 4 4

Colour separations, printing & binding by Tien Wah Press (Pte) Ltd
977 Bukit Timah Road, Singapore 2158

Print supervision by Rodney M Poole

Typeset in Itek Palatino by
Crystal Graphics, 32 Strahan Street,
North Hobart, Tasmania

CONTENTS

Drawings by Peter Jackson

Title-page: below Thunderush, Great Ravine;
p4 and p27: Leatherwood; p7: Aboriginal implements from Kutikina Cave;
p13: Platypus; p14: Portage, Upper Franklin; p15: Huon pine branchlet;
p16: In the rapids, Upper Franklin; p19: Coruscades, Great Ravine;
p21: The Masterpiece; p25: Azure Kingfisher;
p31: Transcendence Reach, Great Ravine.

The Cave

THE CAVE IS HIDDEN from the river. It is hard to find, unless you know just where to look. You have to leave your raft and scramble a short way up the soft bank. Then, through the trees, it opens like a huge, deep fireplace, behind a hearth of fernery. We had come to the wild rivers country looking for something else: a convict skeleton which an old prospector said he had seen long ago in a cave on Goodwins Peak. We searched the slopes of the peak but found no bones. This second cave near the Franklin River was an afterthought. Kevin Kiernan had noticed it five years before and, as we floated past in our rafts, he decided to give it a second look.

A group of grey stalactites hung down from the entrance. Kevin had gone on ahead and his call to us rang with excitement. Ten metres inside was a large mound with a deep pit between it and the cave wall. Kevin was in the pit, his torch set nearby, carefully lifting fragments from the soft, damp mound.

In his hand was a collection of small marsupial bones—some with teeth, some with the unmistakable sockets of hip or shoulder joints—and a few stones. I stooped to pick up another thin, sharp flake of stone and as I handed it to him in the torchlight, I saw Kevin's eyes gleam.

People had lived in this cave. Kevin, Bob Burton and I had disturbed their midden, or fireside rubbish heap, which had remained hidden here for countless years. A few metres away, near the massive middle column of the cave, hundreds of flints lay on the floor. Their razor edges bore the chip-marks carefully worked by the hunters who had made them.

The significance of the find left us speechless. As Kevin and Bob gathered more pieces I moved another ten metres to sit at the back against the rock wall. The cave was warm, roomy, livable. Perhaps the wash of occasional freak floods had removed gathering crusts from the flints which lay clean and dustless on the floor—as if the cave dwellers had just left and were coming back.

I thought I heard a child laugh in the distance. For a moment I saw a group of black people come through the entrance: but it was just the play of sun and shadow from the trees outside. It seemed impossible that centuries had passed since these people left this home. I imagined meeting them and learning from them. But they were gone, never to return.

In the midst of the midden were fragments from the cave roof. Kevin's training as a geomorphologist made him suspect that the cave people had lived there during the last ice age when water in the crevices would have frozen and split away the fragments. Radiocarbon dating has since shown that the midden was deposited between 14,000 and 21,000 years ago. I may as well think of infinity or light years: I cannot grasp the immensity of the time void between us—between my hand and the hand that placed the last stone flint on the cave floor. Kutikina Cave, by the banks of the Franklin, is the southern-most known habitation of people anywhere on Earth during the last ice age.

While the cave was their home and the smoke of their fires billowed up to its roof, the Antarctic ice-sheet stretched to within a few hundred kilometres of Tasmania. Glaciers filled the valleys of the upper Franklin basin and icebergs floated off the coast. Between 10,000 and 25,000 years ago, the freezing seas retreated, opening a land bridge to the Australian continent. Perhaps that led to the arrival of the Kutikina Cave dwellers so long ago. I do not know. Nor do I know why, long before Stonehenge or the Pyramids of Egypt were built, these original Tasmanians abandoned the cave, never to return. But as we left the riverbank near the cave I felt again the yearning to meet them.

We would have had so little in common—except the wilderness environment. For the cave had been there long before those people first took its shelter and the river still flows down its forest-flanked bed, unchanged by their passing or by our arrival at its bank.

Unchanged, so far. How could I have explained bulldozers, chainsaws, turbines and cement to the people of the cave? How could anyone explain submergence of their world beneath 80 metres of dam waters?

As we floated down the last reaches of the Franklin, a platypus surfaced between our rafts. We drew up our paddles and floated on, slowly turning circles while our furred fellow traveller dived and surfaced beside us—just as platypuses have dived and surfaced in this river for millions of years. Again, I thought about the destruction of this wild world. How could I tell this creature, or the forest, or the river itself about bulldozers, chainsaws, turbines and cement?

I couldn't. The only alternative was to tell people back in the towns and cities about platypuses, forests, the river and our own ancestry in wilderness.

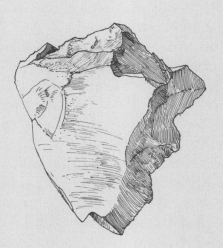

The Land

ABORIGINAL LEGEND tells how the South-West was made by Moihernee. He was hurled down from the heavens after a fight with the great spirit, Dromerdeem. Moihernee "cut the ground and made the rivers, cut the land and made the islands". His wife followed him down to the world and lived in the sea and their children "came down in the rain and went into the wife's womb and afterward they had plenty of children".

Moihernee also overcame some troublesome devils, and made Parlevar, the man. When Parlevar was first made he had a tail and no joints in his legs; he could not sit down. Dromerdeem saw him and cut off his tail, rubbed grease over the wound and cured it and made joints to his knees and told Parlevar to sit on the ground. Parlevar sat down and said it was good.

Scientists explain the South-West differently. They say that when the great ancient continent of Gondwanaland split up, Tasmania and New Zealand were left isolated while the Australian mainland, South America and Antarctica drifted apart on the Earth's surface. Earlier still, over a mind-numbing period of time, shattering earthquakes swept and shuddered through the South-West, giving form to the terrain. The seas, lakes and rivers deposited soft topsoils 1,000 million years ago. Then the tremors and upheavals heated and crushed the soil into all manner of rocks.

Gentler ages followed. Water covered much of the land again, wearing it slowly into another landscape of broad, silty plains. Only the hardest rocky regions jutted above as mountains; the towering crag we call Frenchmans Cap was one. At times great volcanoes flared along the west coast, sending crimson clouds of sulphurous smoke into the sky and molten lavas flowing down to boil the seas. The last great period of upheavals occurred nearly 400 million years ago, say the scientists. They call it the Tabberabberan Orogeny.

The face of the land has changed little since. A short series of eruptions and earthquakes 170 million years ago left columns of solid lava—called dolerite—capping mountaintops such as those we now call Mount Gell and the King William Range, near the headwaters of the Franklin, Denison and Gordon Rivers. The ice ages of the last 2 million years at times dropped the permanent snowline to below 1,000 metres elevation. Then, great glaciers ground down the valleys of the highlands, shaping them to a gentle roundness. The repeated freeze and thaw cracked and shattered the surface rocks of the lowlands, leaving the sharp debris to be swept away in the rush of the spring snowmelt. The rivers continued cutting their courses to the sea, here and there gouging deep gorges through the ranges.

The scientists say that the first people moved to the South-West about 25,000 years ago. In the last ice age the receding oceans exposed a brief landbridge through Flinders Island from mainland Australia to Tasmania. Eight to twelve thousand years ago the ice melted, the seas rose and the landbridge disappeared beneath Bass Strait. For at least 8,000 years the Tasmanian people had no contact with any others. Theirs was an isolation unmatched in the world's history.

So the Aborigines and the scientists have each told their own story. Each stirs the imagination. Each has its own vocabulary of rich and fantastic names. Deep in the gorges of the South-West one can sit today and see the ancient hand of Moihernee cutting a river's path. And high in the mountains a walker can stand looking out over the rows of sawbacked ranges and feel the shocks and tremors of the Tabberabberan Orogeny so long ago.

There are not many places like the wild rivers country left on the face of the Earth: places where the hands of human beings have not obscured the land's origins. Here, the mountains have escaped the scars of roads and the intrusions of powerlines, fences and buildings. The country of the lower Gordon, the Franklin, and the Denison Rivers still breathes free of smothering concrete, bitumen and industry. And so the human beings who come to it can breathe free also.

The wilderness is remarkable. Here the immense volume of the Gordon River's flow is squeezed through the Gordon Splits, a spectacular series of chasms which are, at their narrowest, only six metres wide. Here, along the Denison, Huon pine trees have been growing slowly for two or even three thousand years. And here the Franklin, wild from its placid origins in the high mountain lakes, through its thundering rapid-strewn course to its wide, dark, gentle junction with the Gordon, exists as a living memorial to all the other wild rivers that have been dammed, diverted, polluted, changed.

Perhaps the most remarkable thing about the Franklin–Denison–Gordon wilderness is that it exists. Here and now, in the 1980's, in a far corner of a country covered by the marks of industry, in one of the most technologically-advanced communities on Earth, against all odds, this wild place is still wild.

See the country and see why. The land is so rugged, the cold, wet climate so unrelenting, the vegetation so thick and determined that it has defied humans and their machines. We know the Aborigines lived there, as the glacial icemelt came down the rivers past their caves. They were still visiting the area when the first white people arrived less than two centuries ago. Their food-gathering and fires over millennia may have changed the pattern, but could not destroy the face of the country.

The whites, from the first, came as exploiters. For them, the land was something to be used. Like James Kelly in his open whale boat coming to the mouth of a great freshwater river in 1815, they named the landscape's features for themselves or for the Europeans they knew. Kelly named the river not for its own dark reflections or for the trees that dipped their fronds in its waters or for the animals which dwelt by its banks. He named it Gordon's River, after the owner of his boat.

Kelly was followed to Gordon's River by piners, who came to cut the golden, fragrant, close-grained Huon pines. Then came the prisoners. In 1822, the Gordon River wilderness was a better prison than anything human hands could construct of masonry or metal bars. The surveyor, Evans, who arrived with the first shipload of convicts, reported: "so completely shut in is this

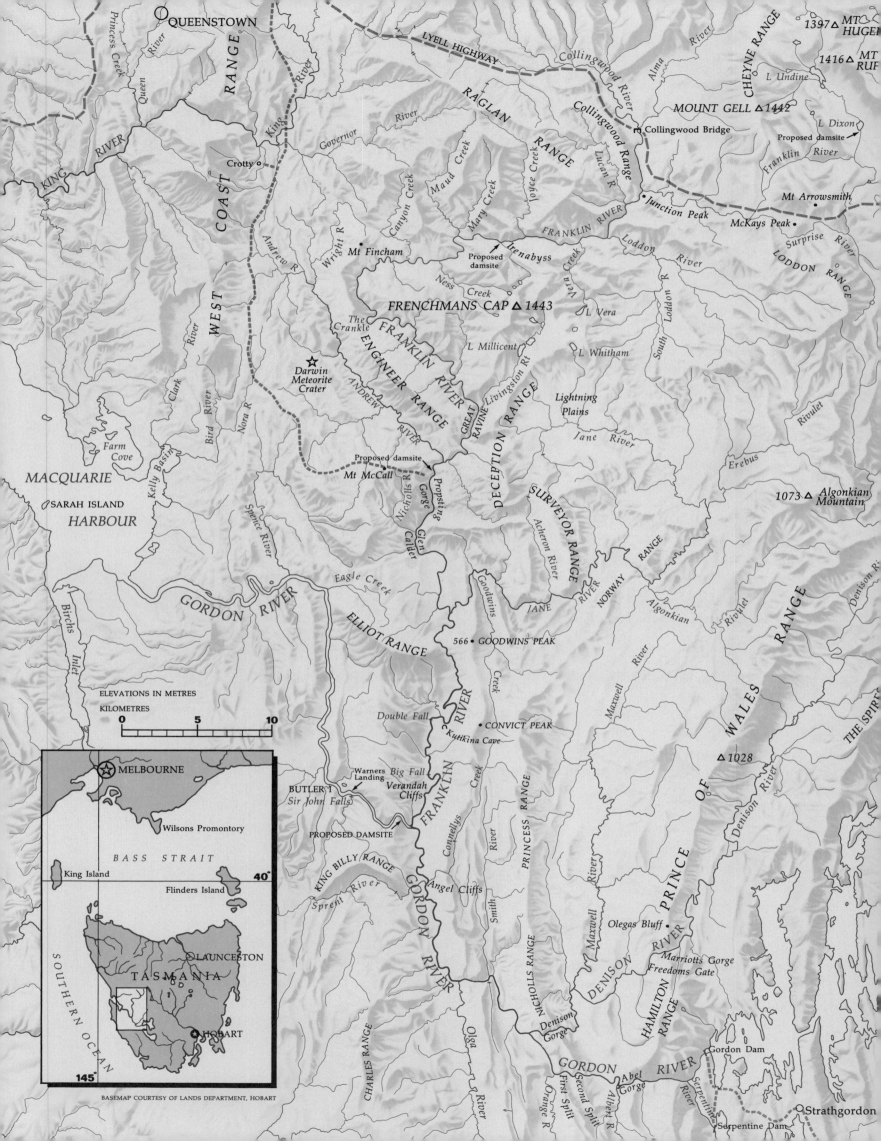

QUEENSTOWN

MT HUGE
1397 △

1416 △ MT RUF

LYELL HIGHWAY

CHEYNE RANGE

MOUNT GELL △1442

L Undine

L Dixon

Collingwood Bridge

Proposed damsite

Franklin River

COLLINGWOOD Range

Collingwood River

RAGLAN RANGE

Alma River

Lucan R

Joyce Creek

Junction Peak

Mt Arrowsmith

McKays Peak

FRANKLIN RIVER

Loddon River

LODDON RANGE

Surprise River

KING RIVER

Princess Creek

Queen River

King River

Governor River

Crotty

Andrew R

Wright R

Mt Fincham

Maud Creek

Canyon Creek

Mary Creek

Ness Creek

Proposed damsite

Irenabyss

Vera Creek

L Vera

WEST COAST RANGE

Clark River

Bird River

Nora R

The Crankle

FRANCHMANS CAP △ 1443

FRANKLIN RIVER

ENGINEER RANGE

GREAT RAVINE

Livingston Rt

L Millicent

L Whitham

South Loddon R

DECEPTION RANGE

Lightning Plains

Jane River

Erebus Rivulet

Darwin Meteorite Crater

ANDREW RIVER

Farm Cove

Kelly Basin

MACQUARIE

SARAH ISLAND

HARBOUR

Spence River

Proposed damsite

Mt McCall

Nicholls R

Gorge Propsting

Glen Calder

SURVEYOR RANGE

Acheron River

1073 △ Algonkian Mountain

Birchs Inlet

GORDON RIVER

Eagle Creek

ELLIOT RANGE

FRANKLIN RIVER

Goodwins Creek

JANE RIVER

NORWAY RANGE

Algonkian Rivulet

RANGE

566 • GOODWINS PEAK

PRINCE OF WALES RANGE

THE SPIRIT

Double Fall

FRANKLIN RIVER

• CONVICT PEAK

Kutikina Cave

△ 1028

Denison River

ELEVATIONS IN METRES
KILOMETRES
0   5   10

Warners Landing

Big Fall

BUTLER T
Sir John Falls

Verandah Cliffs

PROPOSED DAMSITE

Connellys Creek

PRINCESS RANGE

Maxwell River

Denison River

MELBOURNE

Wilsons Promontory

KING BILLY RANGE

Sprent River

GORDON RIVER

Angel Cliffs

Smith River

Olga River

Maxwell River

Olegas Bluff •

Marriotts Gorge
Freedoms Gate

BASS STRAIT

King Island

40°

Flinders Island

CHARLES RANGE

NICHOLLS RANGE

Denison Gorge

DENISON RANGE

HAMILTON RANGE

SOUTHERN OCEAN

145°

LAUNCESTON

TASMANIA

HOBART

First Split

Second Split

Albert R

Orange R

Gordon Dam

GORDON RIVER

Abel Gorge

Serpentine River

Strathgordon

Serpentine Dam

BASEMAP COURTESY OF LANDS DEPARTMENT, HOBART

harbour by the surrounding, closely wooded, and altogether impractical country, that escape by land is next to impossible".

But they did escape—or they tried. Hundreds fled the inhuman conditions of the work camps. Only five of them are known for certain to have made it through the wilderness to settled parts. By 1834 the land and the water had won the first victory against exploitation. The penal settlement was closed. The seas were too rough; the harbour's entrance too hazardous.

In those few years, the only people who knew how to live with the land were destroyed by those who did not. Between 1830 and 1833, the last of the native west coast Tasmanians were rounded up and brought to the penitentiary. In the winter of 1833, eleven of these people died within two weeks. Perhaps a thousand had been living, in harmony with their hard environment, on the south and west coasts in 1804. By 1834 there were none left.

Intractable as the rivers country was, the colonists were reluctant to surrender to it. There were valuable pines there, perhaps minerals, maybe gold. And perhaps there were ways through the wilderness that would make the land's subjugation simpler. For the next fifty years, small parties or lone travellers crossed and recrossed the rivers. The colony's Governor, Sir John Franklin, sent surveyors to find an overland route to Macquarie Harbour at the mouth of the Gordon. In 1842 he set out to see for himself, undertaking, with his wife, a journey of testing hardship. The land won again: no roads were built. Nor were there any mines in the wild rivers country. The prospectors, discouraged by poor results, left to search for eldorados elsewhere.

The piners never really left. Hard-working pining families stayed in the region, cutting and marking the logs and hauling them to the river for the winter floods to carry them down to the harbour. It was a tough life and only a few could face it for long. By the 1960's there were only two families left.

For a few decades, it seemed as if the future would be content to leave the land alone. The tourist sightseers, and a very few adventurers in the 1950's, such as Olegas Truchanas in his kayak on the Gordon, and the Hawkins exploration party canoeing down the Franklin, signalled a new attitude and appreciation of the wilderness. The incredible beauty of the rivers was still there to explore in all its pristine, awe-inspiring splendour. Not to change; not to exploit. Merely to experience and enjoy.

Sadly, by the late 1970's the quiet years were coming to an end. The Tasmanian Hydro-Electric Commission had already penetrated the upper reaches of the Gordon River. By 1972 they had completed one of the most serious assaults ever perpetrated against the world's wild heritage. Beautiful, unique Lake Pedder had been flooded for a power scheme in the midst of bitter controversy, public outcry and political ineptitude.

By the time the Gordon waters began to run cold through the turbines, the hydro engineers had turned their eyes to another set of surveyors' marks on the map of the South-West. Few people knew it, but in the minds of these engineers the last wild rivers were already doomed.

A River Journey

ONE DAY IN 1975 Paul Smith stopped me on the steps of the Launceston Library and asked if I would go with him on a rafting trip down the Franklin River. I said, "Where's that?" I knew almost nothing then of the convicts or the piners or the Hydro-Electric Commission's power plans.

In the weeks before our trip, I learned a little more. Hawkins' 1958 canoe party had reported glass-walled canyons thousands of feet sheer on either side of a torrent so fast it swept craft through without control. In 1972, a four-man party had miraculously survived a trip down the flooding Franklin on a tractor-tube-and-planking raft. The records showed that no one else had followed.

I learned a sketchy geography of our journey. We would start on the Collingwood River where it crossed the highway, and float down to its junction with the Franklin. Two or three weeks and 110 kilometres later, we would reach the point where the Franklin River joins the Gordon and raft down to meet Reg Morrison's *Denison Star*. It was February 1976 when we set off from the Collingwood Bridge, our packs stowed in the bows of our small rubber rafts. The weather was fine, so we were fortunate. Even in summer, the South-West is buffeted by sudden storms and long spells of bleak rain and cold.

As we drifted slowly down the first long reach a platypus silently broke the water's surface. For a few seconds its grey, furred little body floated still, breathing the air, before it dived to forage in a sunken log pile. A long trail of bubbles marked its new expedition to the depths. Three fishermen sat by the second bend, a rifle propped behind them, a beer can apiece. We floated quietly past within touching distance, yet in thoughts no nearer than the planets.

The river now flowed south, away from the road. We drifted by smooth, waterworn rock banks covered in a lush array of moist mosses, lichens and ferns. Overhead, a wide vault of cloudless sky separated the canopies of rainforest. The declining sun came through in places to shine on the river or light the forest floor.

Soon the river converged for a simple, half metre drop between the boulders. It was my first rapid and I remember thinking of Niagara. The rush and fall of it was exciting, frightening. We had expected to camp at the Franklin junction but the wonder of the place and the care with which we took the rapids slowed our progress. Night came quickly. We made a hasty camp on a riverside rockshelf. Rainforest crowded down about us.

In the middle of the night a rock exploded in the embers of the fire. It went off like a shotgun. We sat up, shocked, thinking that someone was upon us. In a few moments I realised the cause of the noise. As I drifted back to sleep I knew that we were far safer in our wild encampment than on the backstreets of any city. In the early morning a soft, thick blanket of mist hung over the river. The thin wisp of smoke from our campfire rose through the foliage of a giant blackwood which leaned out to relax in the open space above the water. Blackwoods, intricate, twisted myrtles and fragrant leatherwoods grew thick and abundant, sheltering an understorey of white-flowered bauera and horizontal scrub. As the first rays of sun broke through the mist and gleamed in myriad lights through the dew-wet leaves, a small tiger snake slithered along the bank. Seeing us, it swam across the river with its head raised a centimetre and its fine black tail brushing the surface as if to smooth away its passing. It crawled out onto a boulder and nestled into a clump of moss in the sunshine.

In mid-morning we met the Franklin. The rivers join in a broad pool dominated by the lofty bulk of Junction Peak. The Franklin emerges from a picturesque canyon to enter the pool between coarse floodpiles of smooth, rounded shingles. It leaves in a long, wide rush of rapids, its volume doubled by the Collingwood.

Back in the Franklin's shadowed canyon, the river seems to emerge from the depths of the mountains. But behind the canyon are miles of high plains. Above those, to the north, are glacial lakes and higher still, are the river's beginnings on an alpine ridge which curves between Mount Gell and Mount Rufus. The waters where we were, at the junction, had already tumbled a thousand metres in altitude from those mountain origins in central Tasmania.

Despite that frosty passage, the sun had warmed the tea-coloured, vegetation-stained water to a temperature comfortable for a refreshing swim.

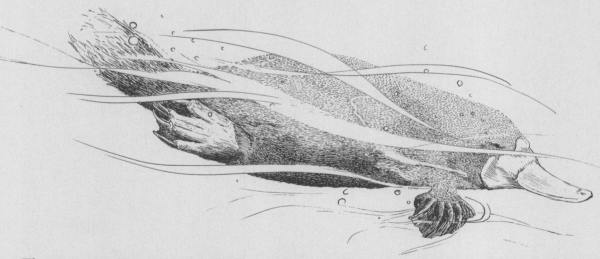

There are only a few weeks each summer when the water is so hospitable. As I floated there, the apprehension I felt in coming to the river vanished. Instead, I felt a deep-down belonging in this place. It engulfed my consciousness. It opened my mind to a natural history and beauty and timelessness which the structure and schedule of urban existence denied. A flock of white cockatoos screeched overhead and vanished behind the eucalypts which lined the brow of Junction Peak. The river rushed on, faster now, deeper now, through steeper country towards the great massif of Frenchmans Cap.

On the morning of the third day we came to a grand old log, anchored on boulders and blocking the river from bank to bank. It could have been there a century; perhaps more.

It held beneath it a dam of smaller logs and branches through which the river spilled in a noisy white commotion.

Next century, perhaps, the log would be gone: finally broken apart by the mighty pressure of some stupendous flood. I wondered how the beautiful pool above it would look then. I tried to imagine the maelstrom in this basin the day the log had lodged after tumbling, booming and crunching, down the narrow corridor of river to crash against these huge boulders. But the Franklin, which usually flowed furiously through these reaches, was running low. The whole river drained below the log and the pool above was still.

Around the next bend the first Huon pines leaned from the Franklin's banks.

Here was a mystery. What makes a Huon pine grow? The first we saw were no stunted, struggling breed: there they were, healthy and strong, their flood-scarred buttresses a picture of permanence. Yet none grow upstream of this point.

Those trees know something we mobile mortals do not. I smiled at our ignorance of the secret.

There, where the Loddon River splashed down a pebbled bed to join the Franklin, we boiled the billy and the marchflies homed in on us—dozens of them. When the sun shone and the billy boiled they always joined us, droning about our heads, landing here and there on our skin.

These giants of the Tasmanian fly family are slow and ponderous and easily flicked away before they lower their chisels to bite for whatever it is they bite.

Sitting there in the sun I spotted a straight edge in the intricate non-conformity of the gravelbank. I went over to pick it out. In my hand was a rusted, pitted file. I didn't know then that prospectors had crossed and recrossed this section of the river at one time, in quest of gold.

WILLIAM TULLY WAS THE FIRST to seek gold here. He came in 1857 and returned in 1859, encouraged by the similarity of the ground to fields he had worked in the rich Victorian gold country. He loved the river scenery with its "ragged outline, and the tortuous ravines". He explored the Collingwood valley which "looked like a park studded with plantations and ornamental timbers". Later, he camped beside the Franklin, below the Collingwood junction, washing quartz gravels and crushing specimens to look for gold specks.

One hot summer morning the fire from an earlier encampment flared. Tully heard a cry from one of his men: "The fire is on us!"

"I saw vast sheets of flame coming down like an avalanche, scarcely one hundred yards distant, and roaring like the sea on a rock-bound shore."

The party made a miraculous escape through the billowing smoke to an already-burnt hill and Tully survived to continue his search. But he found no gold in the wild rivers country.

I have no way of knowing if the file I found was lost by Tully or one of his men but I would have liked to shake the hand that dropped it. I reckoned it was worked by a wise man. No one could spend so much time alone in the bush without learning a lot about life.

Tully would have recognised his 'ragged outline' in the ridges above the shingle bank but his pioneer, prospector's spirit would have been amazed by the rest of the changes a hundred years had brought; the island all mapped, registered and most of it 'owned'. Now the frontiers and wild places had all but gone; on the overcrowded Earth, this Franklin wilderness had become a last refuge. A refuge which would have long since been lost had William Tully's mallet struck gold.

Fire has raged through the bush several times since Tully's near miss. Paul Smith's forester's eye read in the slopes above us the history of recent and ancient fires which had swept the ranges of their once luxuriant rainforests and replaced them with gaunt, charred spars and young eucalypts. Many of the fires started near mining towns far to the west, and were carried here on hot north-westerly gales. The sad spareness of a single King Billy pine skeleton by the river made me wonder if any of the hands which had set alight this wilderness had had any real notion of the vast natural history which their simple actions destroyed.

Near our next campsite stood a magnificent Huon pine which had never been burnt. I looked long and hard into its branches, trying to assess its age. The buttressed base was about five metres around so I guessed that this tree was a vigorous sapling when Christ walked the Earth. Yet its sturdiness spoke of centuries to come.

15

The world closed in on us. Downriver, the gorges became deeper and the forested banks changed to vast, scrub-hung cliffs. I was fascinated by the grey and red river-sculpted rocks and the gentle, diverse greenery. Apprehensive, also, of the 'glass-walled cliffs' to come.

We had been scouting each rapid, pulling ashore to watch the way the water passed around obstructions and to check for submerged logs or sharp stakes which might trap us and drag us under. Here, for the first time, the river narrowed and gained such speed that we could not get ashore to scout ahead.

The view was clear for three hundred metres, but beyond that the river disappeared abruptly beneath a towering bank topped by a vertical cliff. For all we could see the river went straight underground. The river's smooth amber surface broke into a white, frothing maelstrom. We looked at each other, shrugged, and were swept on.

Paul was ahead, his yellow raft bobbing and tossing in the white water. He swept to the left in a powerful shute, then back to midstream among a jumble of boulders. Suddenly, he dropped completely out of sight. I had no control; no choice. Paul had gone, I was going.

As my raft fell through the thundering cascade I glimpsed Paul's red paddle blade. The water spun and pushed me towards him, dropping me through a confusion of noise, rocks and spray.

We washed into a deep, still chasm. There was no gigantic river fall, no sudden disappearance into blackness beneath the cliff. Instead, rock walls folded about the river, narrowing here to a four or five metre gap, widening there to a fifteen metre space. The walls were worn smooth and glistened black in the moist air. Beyond the first pool the sound of the rapids was obliterated. The river's flow slowed to almost nothing: a testimony to the great depths of this narrow, shaded precinct. A wisp of foam from the upstream rapids moved down the corridor tracing a slow, endless pattern of swirls and convolutions. As we floated quietly, turning in circles down the chasm, the silence was broken only by the regular plink of droplets from the walls and the occasional dip and drain of our paddles. In crannies on the cliff walls perfect spider webs, glimmering with moisture, shattered the light into fragments of pure colour.

Later, I found that this beautiful place had no name on the maps and charts of the river. I called it Irenabyss, from the Greek words for 'peace' and 'bottomless'—the Chasm of Peace.

The Irenabyss ends in sudden brightness against a quartzite bank beyond which the creek from Lake Tahune, high on the shoulder of Frenchmans Cap, joins the Franklin in a wide, sunny basin. We watched two grey fantails dart from the branches to flit, insect-snatching, over the pool's surface.

The valley opened out into a way of easy rapids and logjams. For two days we floated west and south where the river made its colossal sweep around Frenchmans Cap. The Cap is Australia's most majestic mountain. It dominates western Tasmania, rising alone from the centre of the Franklin catchment basin. For much of the year it is mantled with snow. It is entirely drained by the Franklin, and mountain and river form a vast natural complement.

THOMAS B. MOORE CAME TO THE CAP in 1887 as an explorer and fossicker. He had been sent to school in the English Lakes District and had developed an abiding love for mountain country. He spent his working life cutting tracks in the South-West of Tasmania. Although untrained, he had the eye of a naturalist and many of the skills of a geologist. His careful studies, sketched at night in lonely camps with only his dogs for company, added much to the early knowledge of the region.

Moore found no precious minerals in the area of the Cap. His expedition's rewards were of a different kind. It was February and he found the river much as we had found it: at a gentle low. A few logs placed across a shallow summer channel allowed him and his companions to cross and continue on to climb the Cap. After several days spent cutting through the tangled horizontal scrub, they arrived at the top, only to find the peak shrouded in mist.

Moore wanted to see the view from the Cap, so he decided "to do a little fasting", camp there for the night and hope for a clear day. He wrote in his diary: "The sun rose gloriously and soon dispelled the clouds from the Cap, and when we reached the cairn one of the grandest and most extensive views met our gaze . . . Took my sights and sketched in rivers, creeks and new prominent mounts . . . Left summit about noon no worse for our fast, and arrived at camp about four o'clock loitering and sorry to leave behind so much loveliness."

Three days later, heavy rain set in and he met with the river's rapidly changing temperament. By the time he got back to the Franklin's bank the river had become a swollen torrent which had carried the log bridge away. With no food to allow them to wait while the river subsided, Moore decided to build a raft of Huon pines.

"Our knapsacks and clothes were placed on board. You can now picture us clad in nature's garb! Walter (Smith) grasping and ready at one corner of the raft, I with the line of straps between my teeth . . . if a photographer could have been on the spot and taken a view of the embarkment and voyage it might have given the general public some slight idea what hardships and dangers an explorer has to undergo in the wilds of Tasmania."

There was little hardship for us, so many years later. Fantastic arrangements of stormclouds crossed the sky, but the rains did not come and the river remained hospitable.

After seven days on the river, and under the serried ranks of the Engineer Range, I gauged that we were at our farthest point from civilisation. I made an initial entry in a small blue diary and hung it, for future travellers, above easy floodreach in a tall myrtle. I knew then that there was nothing so tall as to be beyond the reach of the biggest Franklin flood surge. But the little book did survive to be filled by the growing band of rafters who followed us down the river. On each of my future trips, I found it and recorded impressions of the journey.

*"*W*E OBSERVE THAT IT IS TEA-COLOURED, but we have drunk tea for only a few centuries; we say it is cold or inhospitable or wild, yet it has no emotion or feeling; we call it 'the Franklin' but it flowed for an aeon before Franklin and will flow long after he, like all of us, is forgotten; some set out to 'beat' or 'do the bastard'—meaning this river—but they achieve nothing of that sort nor can they show parentage or scandal in the river's origin; many will pollute these waters though in truth they pollute their own existence and these waters will inevitably, some time, run clear again; many will call it beautiful, love it, hate it, regret their liaison with it or be endeared to it for all of their lives.*

"We are fickle in this personification—fickle and bound in our egos. The river long predated our kind and will flow with us while ever we persist. Its 'patience' will best our pinecutting, dam-building and other transient exploits. And it will continue to flow—past the toxic chemicals, biological mutants or ionizing irradiation which we throw before ourselves to stumble upon—to flow beyond us for more aeons. Oblivious of us and not in any way like us."

Entry Number 2, Tuesday, 15 February, 1977

Just beyond the point where we left the book hanging in its tree, the river snakes and twists like a piece of string around a great 'panhandle' bend which takes it through every compass point within two kilometres. I called this bend the Crankle.

In this region, the diversity of the landscape's character is unending. Each bend brings new vistas as imposing mountains impinge and recede, and creeks cut through narrow gullies or tumble down the mountainside to join the river on its journey south. The exhilaration of the scenery is augmented by the broad open rapids which are frequent and generally safe. We met occasional trouble. My tieline caught on a spar, I was tossed from my raft and

held down by the pressure of a cascade. Buffeted by water, I clung to the raft. Paul edged back up the racing current and passed me his knife to cut the line. Later, he was caught on the unseen snag of a submerged log. Trapped there, the water poured into his raft and swamped him. But after a long struggle, he too managed to float free.

Soon the river narrowed again and the cliffs grew higher and more dramatic. We had entered the Great Ravine, the place of the 'glass-walled cliffs' that had so alarmed earlier parties. We and our craft seemed minute in the immensity of this vast vault of nature. We floated silently down the long entrance pool, looking up in awe at a great frowning buttress which loomed above.

*S*ANDY McKAY HAD NOT COME DOWN THE RIVER. *He didn't even know there was a river there. But what he saw astonished him from his vantage point on the high crags looking down, just as it was to astonish us in our tiny rafts, looking up.*

It was Christmas Eve, 1840. An unforgettable day in the bush, even for Sandy McKay. The only wisp of white in the sky was the morning mist cloud lifting from the top of Frenchmans Cap away to the north. McKay was a scout for the surveyor, James Calder, who was trying to cut a track to Macquarie Harbour. McKay, a former convict, knew a lot about the bush. His skills had won him his freedom in 1828.

On this particular day, he and his two convict companions had walked steadily for four hours to the top of a long range of hills running south and west from the Cap. The view from the top brought disbelief. Instead of a flat, open valley filling the gap before the next range of hills, the terrain fell away from his feet into a tremendous chasm. It was the Great Ravine. Five hundred metres below, the river rushed south.

So much for the track. No path, certainly no road, was possible across this yawning chasm. McKay could neither read nor write and it was left to Calder to describe the impact of the ravine.

The party was camped beneath a huge rock. That night the fireside talk was all of McKay's discovery. But the talk was interrupted by a terrifying lightning storm. The sky flashed white without rain or thunder, giving frozen glimpses of the wild night landscape around them. One tremendous flash set the nearby forest ablaze. The men feared for their safety until a sudden downpour extinguished the flames.

They spent Christmas Day sitting out the rain beneath the shelter which they called Christmas Rock. The next day, Calder went to see the ravine for himself. He wrote: "I tried to lead the road across it at several points, but was thwarted by the intervention of a tremendous ravine. I called these hills collectively Deception Range . . . the great ravine which bounds Deception Range to the westward, is very deep; I dare say two thousand feet; is far too steep for travelling and not to be crossed without excessive fatigue and risk." Twice he scrambled down into the ravine, only to be blocked by "a large and furious torrent . . . I called it the Franklin."

So the furious torrent that blocked McKay and Calder in 1840 became the way itself for us 136 years later. It was not an easy way. Enormous boulders choked the river's course, breaking it into narrow, surging cascades. Passage was impossible. The rafts, packs and our watertight barrels had to be carried precariously across the slippery cliffs beside the river.

Laden with gear, Paul missed his footing on the first of these hauls and fell three metres from a sharp rocky spur. He gashed his back and forearm and bruised his ribs. There could scarcely have been a worse place in which to be injured. There was no way out except the arduous way onward, and there was no way in for rescuers even if they should somehow get wind of an emergency. Luckily, Paul's injuries were slight. With a hot brew and some patching up, his colour soon returned and we moved on.

We floated into the immensity of Serenity Sound, the second and deepest reach of the Franklin in the Ravine. Upstream, a mountain bank stood like a dome and from the rapids at the bend a pattern of white foam coursed down around us on the deep, amber water.

Except for the occasional call of a bird in the forest, there was absolute quiet. For a time the grandeur of this monumental place flooded my mind. I lost awareness of all else—my raft, my friend, my obligations, myself. The process of thirty years which had made me a mystified and detached observer of the universe was reversed and I fused into the inexplicable mystery of nature.

We camped on a low sandbank beneath a lofty southern cliff. Early that morning, a flock of yellow-tailed black cockatoos, the harbingers of bad weather, had swept above us on their way upriver. Now, the rain drumming on our tent proved them accurate forecasters.

Showers swept across the vault through the following day so we stayed tentbound. Paul, still sore and stiff from his fall, was grateful for the day's rest. For all his discomfort, Paul was enjoying the adventure. I had not met him before he asked me to go to the Franklin, but I had heard about him. He had a reputation in bushwalking circles as a dour philosopher, an indwelling and sometimes unruly character. Curiously, the possibility of being caught in the Ravine in a flood both terrified and pleasured him. We were different men: whilst I was spellbound by the beauty of the Franklin, it was clearly the risk and the challenge of the river which excited Paul's mind.

We both greeted the patches of blue between the clouds scudding across the sky the next morning. There were more difficult portages ahead as the river rose, slowly gathering the run-off from the previous day's rain. We moved on and camped further down the Ravine, with the river still rising. As we cooked our dinner, we made bets about how high the rise would be. Before we went to bed the campfire embers steamed and hissed as the river rose to cover them.

But the rise was not great enough to make the river dangerous, and we proceeded through the Ravine for the fourth day to find, at the very end of it, one of the most exquisite campsites on the river. Just upstream, in an alcove beneath the left bank I saw a rock set like an ancient sculpture, its smooth bronzed surface protected from the flood debris which must have frequently

pounded past. Here was a monument to the age of the physical universe. Its solid permanence contrasted with the current sweeping by. I thought of my own transience and that of all life on Earth.

The next morning I went back to watch, deep in thought for an hour, as the sun came over the ridge and lit up the rock in its dark alcove. The 'Masterpiece' shone in bronze brilliance, ageless as the universe: set in contrast with the waters fleeting by like human history.

Just downstream, a creek tumbled through a cranny in the bank and Paul dubbed it the Mousehole. No sooner had he applied the name than we spied a remarkable cat-like rock crouched immediately above the hole. From leather-wood trees on the bank white petals drifted down the still air to land in the river and join us on our passage south into more open country.

*

From beauty and magnificent diversity to deliberate, shocking ugliness: it was just a short, fast run through easy rapids where the Franklin sped south past the entrance of the Andrew River. A rusty file and a few moss-covered pine stumps had been the only marks of man we had seen for twelve days. Suddenly, like a scar slashed across a cheek, the Hydro-Electric Commission's two-rail haulage-way cut through the forest and down the steep face of Mount McCall. At the bottom were drums, plastic pipes and survey marks.

Later I learned that this was the proposed site for a 200 metre high dam. This dam would flood the Franklin back through the Great Ravine and all of the forested Andrew River valley, including the site of the Darwin Meteorite Crater where, some seven hundred thousand years ago a giant molten rock had plummeted past Frenchmans Cap and crashed to Earth, spraying debris as far as Macquarie Harbour. This dam would follow the Gordon-below-Franklin dam which was proposed to flood the lower rivers.

At Mount McCall, I didn't know what the Commission's plans entailed. I just knew that the sight of all that hard, cold geometry in the wilds had triggered an unease in me. It was never to go away.

The haulage-way was more easily left behind: we were soon carried on through more grand gorge country, the thick rainforest and quartzite cliffs on each side of the river hanging out above us at improbable angles. We spent the night on a sloping rock slab which leaned across the river within earshot of the rapids at a place called Rock Island Bend in Glen Calder. As we warmed our hands around our teamugs at dinner, a brilliant display of stars reflected in the river's still black mirror.

We began the next day with a portage around Rock Island's rapids and launched above a series of perfectly formed cascades through which we bounced, dropped and swirled in our rafts to find ourselves in a vastly different Franklin: a river twice as wide, a benign river of gentle banks rather than awesome cliffs, a beautiful river sparkling over shingle stones, shallow and shining in the sun.

*I*T WAS A DIFFERENT KIND OF BEAUTY *Jane Franklin saw when she struggled, wet and fatigued, through the forests to the banks of the Franklin at the place called Glen Calder. Two years earlier Surveyor Calder's party, having been blocked by the Great Ravine, had cut its track south-west to cross the placid Franklin at this ford in a dry, summer spell. But for Lady Franklin, the weather was not fine, and the river was anything but placid. It was a raging, flooding torrent. Rain, hail and snow had buffeted the mountains for days, cascading down to fill the river and push it hard and high against its banks.*

It was 1842. Lady Franklin had scandalised the colony by setting off with her husband, the Governor, on this arduous and perilous adventure. With a woman servant, eighteen male convict porters and five others, Sir John and Lady Franklin left Hobart on horseback in late March. Sir John wanted to use Macquarie Harbour at the mouth of the Gordon River as a penal settlement once again. He hoped to find an overland route that would remove the necessity for the treacherous sea passage from Hobart. They left the horses at Lake St Clair in central Tasmania, and set out on foot, the convicts carrying packs weighing some seventy pounds each. Four of them carried Lady Franklin's palanquin, a chair equipped with carrying rods which was a concession to the proprieties of the day.

Jane Franklin was not much in her chair. The terrain was just too rough. David Burn, a Derwent Valley settler who chronicled the trip in a daily diary of events wrote: "In the roughest and most inaccessible parts she was compelled to wade through miry sludge, or scramble the mountain passes, encamping upon the damp cold ground, the green fern leaves her bedding, blankets her seat, and earth her table. Repeatedly were tents soaked through and through by deluging rain."

After two days they descended Mount Arrowsmith. The Franklin wound away below. They headed west and south to avoid crossing the river. All the time, the rain beat down but the hardship did not blind the party to the beauty of the country: "We were now in the very region of rivers and creeks—that skirts the base of the Frenchman—the beautifully verdant banks and gently swelling slopes surmounted by crags of stupendous height and terrific grandeur", Burn wrote.

Up to their thighs in icy run-off from Frenchmans Cap, they passed flooding waterfalls as thunderstorms swept the region. Finally, "the magnificent Franklin burst upon us—a noble river—by far the largest of any Tasmanian tributary, being, in ordinary seasons, seventy yards of measured width at 'Calder Ferry'. Now, from the very accumulation of mountain torrents, it was a good deal wider, and the body of water immense."

It took the Franklins thirteen days to walk to the river. Their first evening there was fine and the level began to drop quickly. But the rains returned. It was not until nine days later, on the first fine day of the trek, that the party crossed. They used two conjoined, hollowed-out, pine-log 'canoes', hauling themselves by a hawser across the long, smooth reach of the river downstream of Glen Calder. The party walked on to the lower Gordon to meet a ship waiting to take them back to Hobart.

"Our spirits", wrote Burn on the day of the Franklin crossing, "became prodigiously exhilarated, and renovated vigour now infused throughout our weather-beaten, travel-worn frames." Despite the hardship, in his days and nights camped in the forest beside the river, Burn had discovered the Franklin's richest resource. "The ever-varying flood", he wrote, "afforded a vast volume for reflection."

There was time for reflection for us in the days that followed. There were few rapids except the bouncy, shallow races over the red, brown and grey shingles.

The current slowed in these wider reaches and, for the first time, our backs and shoulders felt the strain of paddling, hour after hour through the almost-still broadwaters. Near the rapids, native fish flipped from the surface. In one still pool, the muted blue and yellow of a yabbie clinging to a sunken branch showed through the honey-coloured waters.

The rocks change here too, from craggy quartzite cliffs to the angular folds of grey limestone shot through with veins of white quartz. Some were worn in fluted curves, looking like a stern row of galleons at anchor. Soon we passed the Jane River, named for Lady Franklin. Below this confluence is a wide bank of shingles. The combined current bundled down this bank in a series of waves and troughs which set us whooping at the thrill of the ride.

We pulled left, thinking to repeat the ride the next morning, and made camp in the forest. I lay awake smiling at the scamperings of small animals—wallabies, potoroos and native rats—no doubt flummoxed by the human camp so rudely set across their tracks. In the trees, the ringtailed possums made their quiet chatter and the call of a boobook owl carried through the night.

As we paddled south in the morning the vista expanded. Beyond the limestone cliffs other mountains appeared, range upon range. To the east was a striking peaked hill, clothed to its summit in dense woods, and marked on the map as Goodwins Peak. We made our last camp on the Franklin on a long peninsula of sand which pointed out into the river from a copse of tea-trees on the bank.

A flock of fork-tailed swifts played over the river, rising high and then spiral diving across the waters at astonishing speeds. I had read somewhere that these small birds breed in the Northern Hemisphere and spend their southern season entirely on the wing: they have never been seen to come to land in Australia. Sunset dappled the still waters pink. I watched the darting birds as the light grew dimmer. Suddenly, just before darkness, they were gone.

Not five minutes paddle down the river on our last day on the Franklin, we encountered the twin drops which the piners named Double Fall. The water level was low and we shot through the one metre falls without difficulty. Big Fall, twice as high, waited beyond. To rafters floating down the river, the fall does not at first seem too formidable; but for the piners who named it, hauling their punts upriver, the drop must have seemed big indeed.

Even for rafters, the fall has its hidden difficulties. The drop through space is thrilling but the thrill turns to fear as the water at the bottom turns back on itself, making a mighty stopper wave. It is easy to be trapped there, the water pushing relentlessly back towards the fall, holding the raft and the rafter beneath the torrent. Only furious paddling released us from this unexpected snare. I would not risk shooting it again.

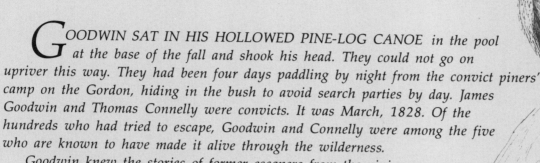

GOODWIN SAT IN HIS HOLLOWED PINE-LOG CANOE in the pool at the base of the fall and shook his head. They could not go on upriver this way. They had been four days paddling by night from the convict piners' camp on the Gordon, hiding in the bush to avoid search parties by day. James Goodwin and Thomas Connelly were convicts. It was March, 1828. Of the hundreds who had tried to escape, Goodwin and Connelly were among the five who are known to have made it alive through the wilderness.

Goodwin knew the stories of former escapers from the pining camp. He knew of Alexander Pearce and his wretched companions who had fled the known horrors of the penal settlement to confront the even greater horrors of hunger and cannibalism in the unknown wilderness. Goodwin made his plans carefully: he would try to keep to the rivers rather than the dense forests, he had a compass and he spent weeks stashing supplies from his meagre bread and meat rations. In secret, he hollowed out a Huon pine log to make a large, crude canoe. Goodwin and Connelly waited till the pining gang was away from the riverside, dashed to their canoe, loaded their stores and swiftly paddled upstream.

Near dawn of the second night they passed Butler Island, a rocky crag which stood like a ship in mid-river. As the sun rose they paddled on and by midday they had reached the then-unnamed Franklin River.

Soon they were hauling their boat up the first pebbly rapids, past the limestone cliffs and caves, exhausted and no doubt dogged by fears of hostile natives and tigers stalking the bush. They were free, but they faced a challenging prospect: they had to cross the wild western half of Tasmania before they had any hope of reaching a settlement.

When they reached Big Fall, Goodwin knew his plan to use the rivers was finished. This fall was probably the precursor of even greater drops upriver. They tied their craft to a tea-tree and struck out for the mountain to the north-east, now called Convict Peak, just south of Goodwins Peak.

They struggled through some of the thickest bush in Australia—cutting-grass, tangled tea-trees and criss-cross horizontal trees. They were tough men in their late twenties, hardened by the exertion of long days hauling logs, often chest-deep in water even in the frigid winter months. They were courageous and intelligent, and determined to reach freedom.

To do it, they had to swim the Maxwell and Denison Rivers, cross the jagged Prince of Wales Range and the snow-covered flank of Wylds Craig, from which they finally descended, three weeks after their escape, into the settled Derwent Valley.

They rationed their food carefully "as we did not fall in with anything we could eat". In the Derwent Valley they were fed by shepherds, and Connelly set out alone for New Norfolk. He was never recaptured.

Goodwin was captured near Ross in the Midlands. But his knowledge of the mysterious South-West and his proven ability as a bushman saved him from the gallows or a return to the hardships of the Macquarie Harbour penal settlement.

As Goodwin and Connelly had paddled upstream, so Paul and I paddled down, heading for the beautiful expanse of Macquarie Harbour that to them had been a prison. Knowing that our adventure was soon ending, and reluctant to leave the river, we spent some time exploring the limestone caves.

Most were shallow, but others we withdrew from before fully exploring, because we could not be sure of our footing in the absolute blackness of their depths. On that first trip, we floated right past Kutikina Cave and its secret human history. One giant cavern opened to the river and we floated into it on the creek which wound through its floor.

Near the overhang of Verandah Cliffs I took aboard two large polished rocks and promised myself that one day, when this region was safe from the man-made disaster it now faced, I would return them to the river.

It was late in the day when we floated out of the Franklin and headed west down the mighty Gordon. The forest-clad hills stood high on all sides. I thought of the piners who had worked these rivers for more than a century. I wondered about the distant Gordon Splits, and about the legendary Angel Cliffs which I knew to be not far up the Gordon. The ancient Angel, a calcite embossment on a lofty grey limestone cliff, had been the piners' 'guardian'.

REG MORRISON WAS JUST FIFTEEN when he left Strahan to join a pining gang in the mid-1930's. He often passed beneath the Angel and grew to believe that anyone who destroyed it would meet with ill-fortune. For the piners it was a unique, sacred presence in the heart of the rivers region. Maybe the Angel had sway when Reg and his brother Ron achieved the 'impossible' in 1940. They hauled their pinewood punt up the Franklin through Deception Gorge—the complex gorge system from Glen Calder to the Great Ravine—to a camp beneath Mount Fincham. It was the first passage of the gorge in history.

The Morrisons were fit young bushmen, hardened by the task of felling and hauling Huon pines and then floating them down the rivers. They worked in rain, hail or shine, and mostly it was rain. They lived in the forests for weeks at a time. At night they sheltered in tents or pineslab huts, sleeping on chaffbag-and-poles bunks.

In the late 'thirties the Morrisons cut a track overland past Mount Fincham to the Franklin. Older piners said the Franklin gorges were impassable: a huge waterfall, hundreds of feet high, blocked passage through the central gorge. To meet this hazard, Reg and Ron decided to come upstream from the Gordon.

Fortune was with them. It was March, the river was low and the sunny weather held. For provisions they had half a bag of potatoes, the same of flour and a side of bacon. They also carried a camp oven, crosscut saw, ropes, axes, a tin of kerosene, tent and bedding. Every night they cooked fresh damper.

They dragged their punt over every rapid, deep into the Ravine. While the legendary waterfall did not eventuate, the passage of the rapids was an astonishing feat. In one 'ticklish operation' the men hauled the lot vertically up a one-hundred-foot cliff. At another spot, probably Thunderush rapid, they would have failed except for a log caught up against a huge boulder; the log gave their ropes leverage to haul the punt over the boulder while the rapids thundered around. The punt sank beneath another section of cascades. Miraculously, after hours, just as the men prepared for a scramble out of the Ravine, the punt broke free of the downpour and bobbed to the surface.

On the sixteenth evening, ten days late and while a search party was gathering at Strahan, Reg and Ron Morrison reached their camp at Mount Fincham.

When Paul and I paddled out of the Franklin onto the Gordon, we did not know that exactly thirty-six years earlier the Morrisons had rowed their punt in the opposite direction. But while the Franklin had not altered in those years, the Gordon had.

At once, I sensed something was wrong. The Franklin River is warm and alive, its waters heated by the sun as it flows free from the mountains. The Gordon is icy. Its waters now flow down as the Hydro-Electric Commission wills, through concrete and turbines, from the bottom of cold, black Lake Gordon. A mist rose from the surface where the warm water mingled with the cold. Cold water, cold sound: jackhammers shattered the silence, ripping into the hillside.

We had come to the site of the Gordon-below-Franklin dam: a giant rock-fill wall would stop the river's free flow here and back it up to flood all of the lower Franklin, right up to Mount McCall. The Franklin dam there, and yet others planned for the Irenabyss and at Lake Dixon in the highlands, would complete the Franklin valley's destruction.

I didn't know it then, but this first dam's reach would also extend back up the Gordon, over the Angel Cliffs, into the Denison River valley and the Gordon Splits beyond Sunshine Gorge—all priceless, ancient, extraordinary places, part of one of the world's finest tracts of wild and scenic heritage.

We settled into our last camp, upstream of Butler Island. The next day we would paddle down to meet Reg Morrison's *Denison Star*. Two brilliant blue kingfishers darted from their perches in the scrub, snatching their meal from the dark waters. They did not seem to notice our presence, nor even that of the Hydro-Electric Commission's helicopters and motor boats grinding and droning through the Gordon's primeval quiet. The journey down the Franklin had been the best fourteen days of my life. Now I felt sick at heart.

The Challenge

TASMANIA'S WILD RIVERS are a litmus for the world. If, in this peaceful and lucky corner of the planet, we cannot save these rivers, surely the world itself is beyond rescue from the greed and short-sightedness of human affairs.

The challenge to save the Franklin, Denison and Gordon Rivers involves more than a question of wilderness. It is a challenge to overcome entrenched bureaucracies, selfish politics and human apathy. It is a challenge to rein in the age of technology and materialism before it bolts away and carries us all to despair and destruction.

It is a challenge to put concern for our fellows and our fellow creatures in a pre-eminent place; to respect both the past generations who lived with nature and the generations who will follow us in search of natural beauty. It is a challenge to have these concerns put before dollars, megawatts and the short-term self-interest of those who would destroy the last wild and scenic places.

I once stood by the wild wooded shores of Lake Undine in the Franklin high country. It was a clouded, gloomy day. Snow-covered ranges rose up from around the lake. To the south, the valley opened to buttongrass plains through which the river meandered toward Lake Dixon and the rough, rocky gorge beyond. I had left three companions sitting in the woods. They were listening to the waves lapping on the pebbly shore and talking about the glaciers which once filled the valley.

Except for the waves and the mountain wind, all was quiet. I noticed a blaze on a tree and wondered who had cut it. It looked half a century old. Suddenly, from a break in the lowering clouds, a bolt of sunlight hit the snowbank on the ridge high above me. It swung across the ridge bringing brilliance to the cliffs and boulders, the snow and trees. Then, just as suddenly, the beam was gone and the ridge fell back into gloom.

Nature is infinite. The universe is a limitless repository of events. No one will ever see that bolt of sunlight on the ridge as I saw it, nor will they feel what it did to my soul. Others will have a coat like mine, will ride in similar cars down similar highways, watch the same television programmes, sit in the same city squares. But no one, not even I, will ever experience anything like my moment by Lake Undine again.

We city-bound human beings are apt to forget that we are part of nature. Deep in all of us is a strong bond with the rest of the natural universe; and especially with the Earth. No wonder. Until the last blink of history, our ancestors spent millions of years as part of the wild world. So our minds and bodies were adapted for a wilderness existence.

Then came the industrial and technological revolutions. The face of the globe has been drastically altered. At the start of this century most of the landscape was wilderness. Now most is not. And as the remaining patches of wilderness are being eroded, the rate of their destruction is accelerating.

Clearly, technology has brought great benefits to the human community.

Just as clearly, it is out of control and heading us for needless hardship and harm. The rushed, short-sighted and extravagant marauding of nature is only the immediate result of this tearaway technology. The most singularly fearful result is the worldwide stockpiling of nuclear, chemical and other weapons which now threatens all life on Earth. These things stem from the human community's failure to balance its technological prowess with restraint, compassion and concern for the Earth's future. So the fight to save the last of the wilds is more than a fight for heritage, it is part of the struggle to ensure human survival itself.

We need wilderness. The concrete canyons, asphalt plains and plastic flowers of the modern city are no substitute for nature's wide open spaces. Future generations will live in even more populous and stress-ridden communities. For them, even more than ourselves, those refreshing tracts of wild country will be oases in a desert of machine-made landscapes.

Mostly, like many city folk today, they will prefer to walk on level concrete rather than to scramble barefoot over rocks and tussocks; to reach for refreshment across a counter rather than to the mossy edge of a stream; to recline on an electric blanket rather than side by side with twenty naked others in a cave-floor huddle. Mostly. But who would live in an entirely synthetic landscape without ever the chance to wander free in the wilds? Who would take from their children forever the chance to experience the natural world of our ancestors—or even the excitement which comes from knowing that such places exist? Wilderness is peace of mind. In destroying the last of it we will gain nothing of lasting value yet lose a vital heritage and even, perhaps, ourselves.

The plan to dam the wild rivers of South-West Tasmania embodies nearly everything which is wrong with 'progress' in this age of amazing technological capabilities. These priceless, pristine precincts speak for themselves to any sensitive and humane intellect. Nothing warrants their destruction.

Nevertheless, it is worth a brief look at the other arguments used by those who demand the Gordon-below-Franklin dam. The arguments for the second or Franklin dam are almost identical, by the way. The Gordon-below-Franklin dam would produce an average of only 180 megawatts of electricity. In engineers' jargon, it will have an installed capacity of 296 megawatts in peak periods. It matters little which figure is used. By comparison, Victoria's Loy Yang thermal power station will have a capacity of 4,000 megawatts. Canada's La Grande hydro-electric scheme will produce over 13,000 megawatts. So Tasmania's government, at the behest of its Hydro-Electric Commission engineers, intends to destroy the heartland of the South-West wilderness for a pittance of power. The small Tasmanian community would have to pay more than one thousand million dollars for that to happen. And the project would employ an average of less than 600 people during its ten years of construction: then just 29 for its long-term maintenance. The same money would, of course, employ thousands more people if invested in labour-intensive pursuits attuned to Tasmania's long-term needs without threatening its internationally renowned wilderness.

Meanwhile, the need for that 180 megawatts—if it ever existed—has gone. Tasmania's heavy industries have cancelled expansion plans. The 200 megawatt Pieman River scheme in the island's north-west, a five-dam *fait accompli* by the H.E.C., is coming on line with enough electricity to supply Tasmania's new needs till near the end of the century. The H.E.C.'s 1979 predictions of growth in demand for electricity were wrong. In fact, by 1982, there was a decline in Tasmania's estimated use of electricity. Whichever way it is viewed, the wild rivers scheme is absurd, unforgivable. It is a travesty of common sense.

Despite the travesty, the nineteen men in government and the engineers of the H.E.C. have ordered the bulldozers and chainsaws to move in. The living wilderness faces death and destruction. Forever. Sight unseen. The Premier of Tasmania has not been to see the Franklin's Great Ravine, Glen Calder or Kutikina Cave, the Gordon Splits or Angel Cliffs, or Freedoms Gate on the Denison. Nor has he stood to marvel beside the ancient Huon pines in the threatened riverside rainforests.

Recently, while explaining that he had never been there, the Premier said of the Franklin River: "For eleven months of the year it is nothing but a brown ditch, leech-ridden and unattractive to the majority of people". Reckless and primitive as such a sentiment in government may be, it led to the 'go-ahead' for preliminary work on the scheme. For the time being, these works are proceeding.

Yet it would take a decade for the project to reach its most devastating climax: for the diversion gate to be shut and for the dam to begin filling. Time enough for the project to crumble under a growing flood of informed concern and opposition.

Ultimately, the future of the world as well as this wilderness relies on optimism, action and determination by thoughtful people—even in the face of repeated adversities. It is now apparent that saving the rivers means enduring the early transmogrification of some of the downstream region. One of the world's oldest national parks, the Lower Gordon Scenic Reserve, is an early target for roads and worksites. The Reserve was set aside in 1908 and draws over 60,000 visitors annually on cruises to beyond Butler Island. It is one of the world's last wild river regions frequented by sizable cruise vessels. The western flank of the lower Franklin is also listed for early despoliation.

Confronted with this appalling spectacle we will be expected to give up. We will not. Too much is at stake. There is too much to win.

Already thousands of Australians have come to the rivers' aid by writing letters to politicians and making donations or working with the Tasmanian Wilderness Society and its fellow conservation groups. Hundreds of thousands have made 'no dams' write-in votes at elections or joined in public rallies across the country to protest at the impending destruction. Polls show that a massive majority opposes the dam.

In 1982 the wild rivers region and nearly half of the rest of the South-West was officially inscribed on the World Heritage List. It is one of only thirty regions to have gained this recognition for their natural significance to the world. The List is drawn up under the auspices of the World Heritage Convention of UNESCO in Paris. Under the Convention, which Australia signed in 1974, the Federal Government in Canberra is obliged to 'do all it can' to stop the dam. It has the power to intervene in Tasmania, on behalf of the nation, to save the wild rivers region—and the Convention requires that it do so.

International opposition to the dam is growing as pressure on the Federal Government mounts. Almost incongruously, modern technology is giving vital assistance. Film, photographs and news of the threatened rivers is being transmitted far beyond the South-West itself. At home, in their living rooms, people are watching as the tragedy unfolds. The progress of the H.E.C.'s heavy machinery will be seen by countless people for however long it takes to halt. The campaign to stop the dams has brought together many caring and enthusiastic people. The ranks of the river defenders grow while the pro-dam lobby, although in power in Hobart, has exhausted its growth.

The Earth will be a better place for the South-West wilderness: for the rhythm of life in its riverside forests; for the mystery and human heritage of its caves; for the peace and gentleness of its wide river reaches; for the thunder of the torrents echoing through its gorges.

These living, wild places face death and destruction from men and machines. They cannot defend themselves. The onus is ours. We are challenged to stop that destruction, however great the effort, however soon we can.

PHOTOGRAPHS

Peter Dombrovskis

Ecological Notes by Dr Jamie Kirkpatrick, University of Tasmania

Franklin Headwaters

WHERE THE LAND rises more than 1200 metres in central Tasmania and fire has been excluded by dampness, isolation and the barriers of cliff and scree slope, the landscape has the aspect of a garden. On the undulating upper slopes of the Cheyne Range every second plant species has a natural distribution that is confined to Tasmania. Every third or fourth plant species has its closest relatives not in Australia, but in the scattered lands of the far south of the globe. To find other deciduous southern beech *(Nothofagus)* species such as *N. gunnii* it is necessary to visit the mountain forests in the south of South America.

The creeping pine *(Microcachrys tetragona)* is found in Britain as a prized rockery shrub, but is native only to the highlands of Tasmania where its red succulent cones are eagerly devoured by the black currawong *(Strepera fuliginosa)*. Similarly confined to Tasmania are the pencil pine *(Athrotaxis cupressoides)* and several species of the hard, green mounded cushion plants. The deciduous beech, the various native pines and the cushion plants dominate vegetation complexes that have been destroyed elsewhere in Tasmania by fires lit by unthinking European man. The Cheyne Range is one of the few mountains where the alpine and subalpine vegetation still exists unscarred.

The slow percolation of mountain water through heath, pool and bog coalesces into rapid mountain streams which tumble down steep slopes to flow into lakes Undine and Dixon, on the flat floor of a valley once filled by glacial ice. Permanent ice disappeared from Tasmania some nine thousand years ago but will probably return, as it has many times in the past.

The retreat and dissolution of the glaciers saw an advance of the characteristic button grass *(Gymnoschoenus sphaerocephalus)* sedgelands which occupy poorly drained areas in lowland western Tasmania. Eucalypts and rainforest species also returned, their mixture and juxtaposition in both life and lichen-encrusted death creating a landscape of great ecological complexity.

Tasmania's Hydro-Electric Commission considers Lake Dixon to be a future damsite with the potential of producing four megawatts of electricity.

ICICLES ON CREEPING PINE, CHEYNE RANGE

CUSHION PLANTS AND PENCIL PINES, CHEYNE RANGE

DECIDUOUS BEECH AND LICHENS

MOUNT HUGEL RISES BEYOND A PINE-RIMMED LAKE, CHEYNE RANGE

MORNING AT LAKE DIXON

LICHENS ON DEAD EUCALYPT, LAKE DIXON

EUCALYPT BOLE AFTER RAIN, LAKE DIXON

REEDS AND EUCALYPT LEAVES, LAKE DIXON SHORELINE

FRANKLIN RIVER, LAKE DIXON

Middle Franklin

BETWEEN the lakes of its upper reaches and the Great Ravine, the Franklin receives water from numerous mountain catchments, almost all deep in wilderness. Where it joins the Collingwood River the Franklin becomes large. Upstream of the junction it flows as a stream of shallow rapids and deeper pools between mountain slopes clad with tall alpine ash *(Eucalyptus delegatensis)* and emerald rainforest. Below the junction it sweeps westward forty kilometres through a land of gorges and scrub-covered slopes.

The scrub, consisting of dense, pole stands of Smithton peppermint *(Eucalyptus simmondsii)*, narrow-leaved wattle *(Acacia mucronata)*, shiny tea-tree *(Leptospermum nitidum)* and paperbarks *(Melaleuca species)* with impenetrable understories consisting of bauera *(Bauera rubioides)* and cutting grass *(Gahnia grandis)* is a post-fire replacement of rainforest, which survives only as small patches in gorge and riverside.

When floodwaters slow they deposit sand and gravel, locations occupied by delicate riverine herbs, some of which are confined to such places and several of which are also Tasmanian endemics. Shaded rocks are covered by mosses and herbs such as oxalis *(Oxalis lactea)*, and shaded banks by moss and fern. However, the same floodwaters scour many places clean and their load of soil particles and stone smooths jagged rock into a gemstone finish. The oxidation of impurities in the quartzite gives a ruddy glow to rocks protruding from the rush of tannin-stained water. Its power churns pebbles and rocks trapped in hollows until, centuries later, deep potholes form.

In the Irenabyss the water runs twenty metres deep and in flood rises twenty more, creating a zone of bare rock much taller than where the river runs wide. Down the long, deep corridor traceries of foam drift on the slow surface current and tell of the turbulent rapids in the gorge upstream.

The Irenabyss gorge has been indicated as a future damsite in the proposal to fully develop the Franklin's potential for power production. Above the peaceful surface of the chasm black cormorants *(Phalocrocorax carbo)* fly, in air that would become stagnant water if the dam were built.

FRANKLIN RIVER AT PINE CAMP

SUMMER CASCADE, FRANKLIN RIVER

FERNS AND PEBBLES IN A RIVERSIDE ALCOVE

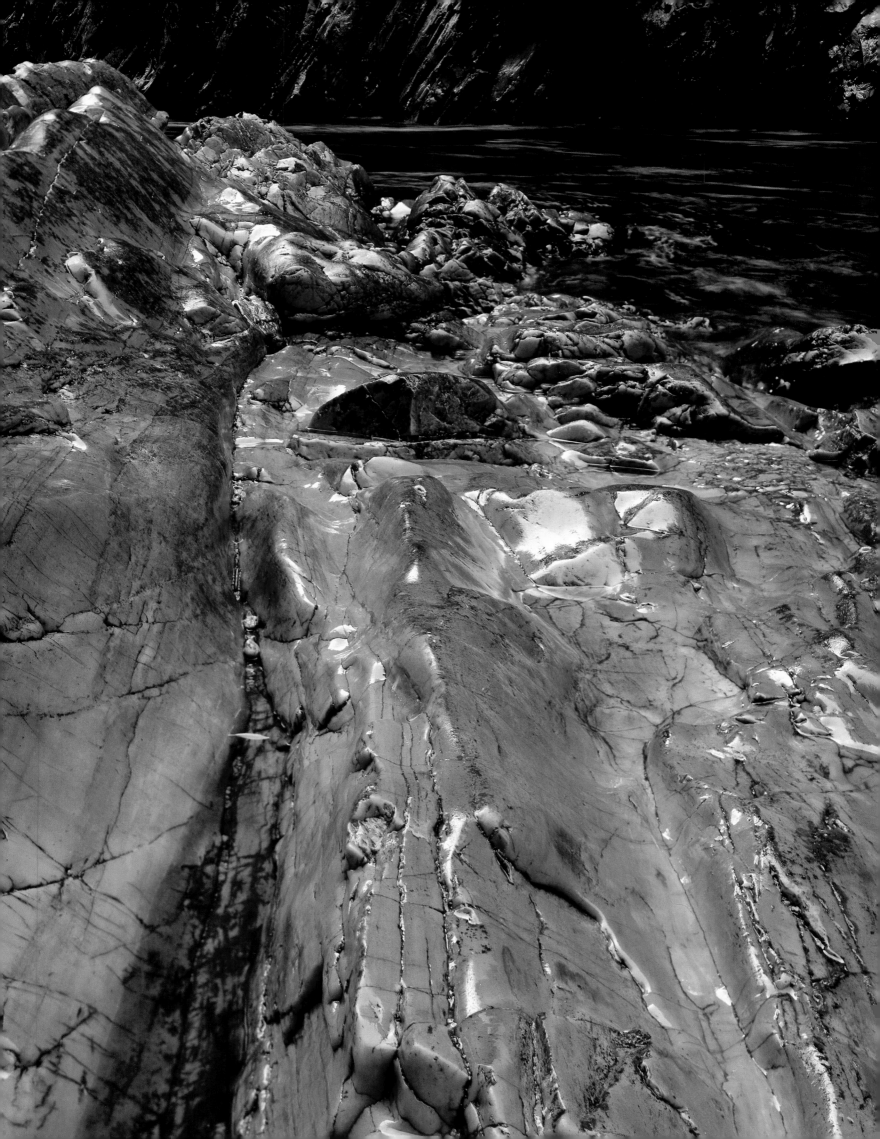

ROCK AND RAPID BELOW PINE CAMP

POLISHED QUARTZITE ABOVE IRENABYSS

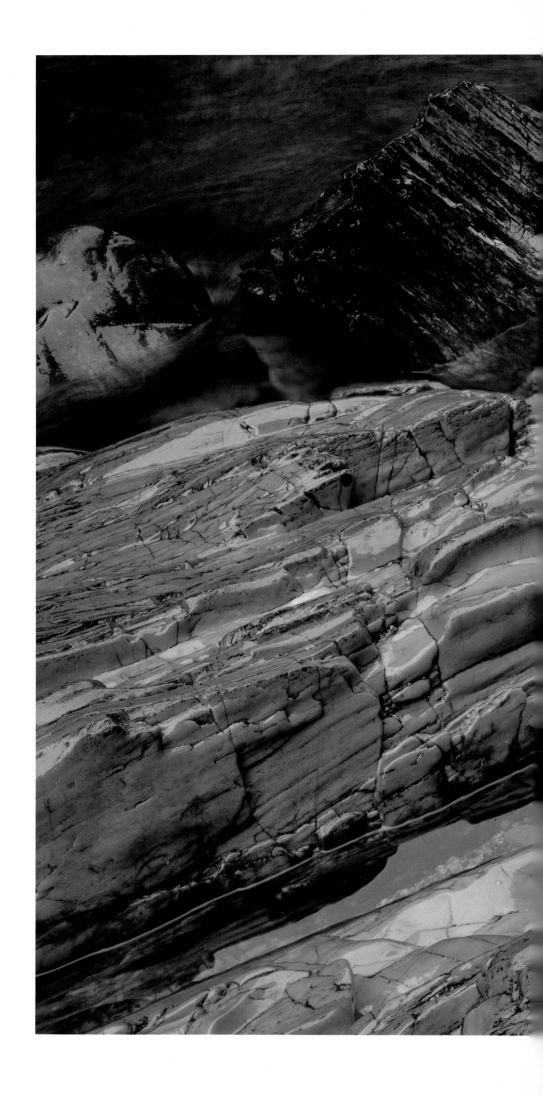

POLISHED QUARTZITE ABOVE IRENABYSS

Great Ravine

THE GREAT RAVINE is the largest gorge in Tasmania, extending for ten kilometres with its rims up to five hundred metres above the large river below. In the heart of the Great Ravine the Franklin falls through the Churn, Coruscades, Thunderush and Cauldron. Between these boulder-strewn rapids the river flows quietly beneath towering banks and buttresses in broad, open reaches. The deepest-set stretches of calmer water—Serenity Sound, Transcendence Reach and the Sanctum—are often lost beneath the mist-shrouded mountains. Cascades arising in the hidden peaks above spill from overhanging ledges and striate the walls.

The precipitous slopes support forest with an increasing component of temperate rainforest species, the Huon pine *(Lagarostrobos franklinii)* being an occasional streamside tree or shrub. The river floods in any month and the ravine walls are swept almost clear of vegetation to fifteen metres above low summer level. Where there is room, piles of driftwood mark the floodtime eddies and sometimes give rise to makeshift ferneries—until the next violent surge arrives.

Directly to the north, and almost 1400 metres above is Frenchmans Cap, one of the most outstanding features of the South-West wilderness. In an inconspicuous valley to the east of Frenchmans Cap and the Great Ravine a large meteor once fell, scattering in the heat of collision a substance called Darwin glass. The accumulation of pollen in the peats that have subsequently filled this crater may provide evidence of many tens of thousands of years of vegetation change.

On the ridge of Mount McCall, and highly visible from Frenchmans Cap, the white scar of a road extends to the Franklin. The quartzites of the west resent disturbance, their glare being effectively permanent as almost all plant nutrients are contained in the peat and vegetation. Between the ironically adjacent Engineer and Deception Ranges, the Great Ravine awaits inundation from the dam planned for the end of this road, a dam that would also flood the Darwin Meteorite Crater. The romantic associations of mist and mountain, floodwood and fern, cascade and chasm would be submerged to a depth of 120 metres or more.

SERENITY SOUND FROM TOP OF CORUSCADES, GREAT RAVINE

THUNDERUSH RAPID, LOW SUMMER LEVEL

TRANSCENDENCE REACH, GREAT RAVINE

FERN AND ROCK NEAR THUNDERUSH

THE SANCTUM, GREAT RAVINE

ABOVE THE CAULDRON, GREAT RAVINE

Glen Calder

THE FIRES that converted rainforest to scrub along much of the middle reaches of the Franklin did not reach the last of the Franklin gorge country, Glen Calder. The Glen is a moist, misty place of boisterous rapids, dripping greenery and hidden waterfalls.

The Tasmanian temperate rainforest is richer in moss and lichen species than in higher plants. These lower plants cover rock, soil and trunk of myrtle *(Nothofagus cunninghamii)*, sassafras *(Atherosperma moschatum)*, leatherwood *(Eucryphia lucida)*, horizontal *(Anodopetalum biglandulosum)*, celery top pine *(Phyllocladus aspleniifolius)*, Huon pine and other smaller tree and shrub species. The bizarre palm-like pandani *(Richea pandanifolia)* is a heath which can gain the canopy of the elfin, tangled rainforest. Elsewhere, the floor of the rainforest can be a shaded park with straight-boled trees and long green views, occasionally interrupted by the umbrella of a man fern *(Dicksonia antarctica)*.

The interdependence of different species is seldom more evident than in rainforest, where the closed canopy of trees creates the constantly humid, cool and shaded environment necessary for the delicate filmy ferns and other hygrophytes. Here, the root systems of trees often fuse and the very soil that supports the forest can consist of the accumulation of red, fibrous peat from the litter of hundreds of generations of trees. If fires gain access to this organic soil on the few days each year that it is dry, the consequences are disastrous, unburned trees collapsing with the loss of their supporting soil.

More usually, the soil is saturated and the low cliffs and tea-tree breaks scattered along the riverside are frequently submerged by furious floods. Once a year or so floodwaters hurl their flotsam down the corridor of Glen Calder at the buttress of Rock Island which rises defiantly from mid-river. Only the copse of scrub atop the Island is left above the foam, and not even that when the biggest flood crests arrive. Beyond the Island the Franklin falls fifteen metres down the bedrock staircase of Newland Cascades.

The riverine rainforests would be killed and drowned and the whole of Glen Calder permanently inundated if the Gordon-below-Franklin dam were allowed to be built.

TRIBUTARY STREAM, GLEN CALDER

FEEDER ROOTS AND MOSSES, GLEN CALDER

WATERFALL AT ROCK ISLAND BEND, GLEN CALDER

MORNING MIST, ROCK ISLAND BEND

RAINFOREST FUNGI, GLEN CALDER

PORTAGE TRAIL, ROCK ISLAND BEND

Lower Franklin

DURING THE LAST GLACIAL, remnant ribbons of rainforest sheltered and survived along the banks of the lower Franklin. As the air grew warmer and moister and the ice retreated, the forest species spread and flourished again. The surrounding country was open and covered by alpine vegetation, and people occupied caves by the river.

Formed in limestone over 400 million years old, the caves are the product of western Tasmania's cool wet climate and acidic groundwater. In these conditions limestone dissolves more easily than almost all other rocks. Thus, it forms the valleys rather than the hills as in the tropics. When the overlying rocks were removed by erosion, the release of pressure caused the limestone beds to crack, allowing moisture to percolate down and along the joints and beds. The lower Franklin and Gordon River valleys are rich in caves, with major archaeological discoveries being made each year.

The long, colourful shingle banks also carry a tale of harsher times. These gravels come from the outwash of highland glaciers. Their long journey to the lower reaches of the Franklin has ground them smooth and round. But the fine sand, which in places forms smooth banks, is the work of water rather than ice.

The vegetation now is tall rainforest with some blackwood (Acacia melanoxylon) component where flood damage or large tree falls have created the conditions necessary for its establishment. Some of the rarest plant species in Tasmania are found on the limestone cliffs, including a beautiful, white-flowered, long-leaved lily, Milligania longifolia.

Today's fauna is only slightly different from that documented by bone and carapace in the formerly occupied caves. Few of the animals are dangerous to man. Even the three venomous snake species found in the region are aggressive only with due cause. Marsupials are shy, with the notable exception of the possum, and are not often seen, although a wealth of bird species is some considerable compensation for the general lack of visible large mammals. Trout compete in the river with the native fishes, but few other introduced species are found.

This area, with all its life and beauty, would be obliterated by the Gordon-below-Franklin dam.

LOWER FRANKLIN BELOW JANE JUNCTION

VALLEY FOG DISSIPATES BELOW ELLIOT RANGE

LIMESTONE OUTCROP AND FLOOD DEBRIS NEAR GOODWINS PEAK

ERODED LIMESTONE, VERANDAH CLIFFS

VERANDAH CLIFFS, LOWER FRANKLIN

ERODED LIMESTONE, VERANDAH CLIFFS

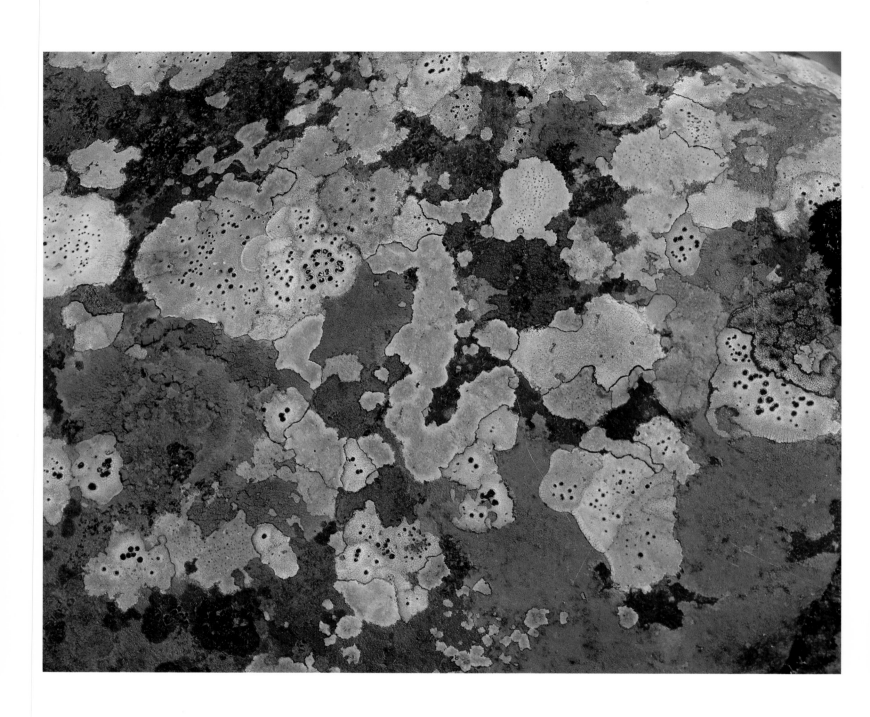

LICHEN-ENCRUSTED BOULDER BELOW NEWLAND CASCADES

SLOUGHED SNAKESKIN BELOW NEWLAND CASCADES

FLOOD-SCARRED RIVER TEA-TREE, LOWER FRANKLIN

Denison River

RISING in the heights of the King William Range, the Denison River has its source just south of the origin of the Franklin. For much of its eighty-five kilometres the Denison parallels the jagged and narrow Prince of Wales Range, winding through a corridor of rainforest flanked by open scrub and button grass plains.

At the northern end of the Hamilton Range the river parts company with the Prince of Wales through Marriotts Gorge. Freedoms Gate is a deep cleft between pincer-like spurs at the downstream end of Marriotts Gorge. The boulder-choked Denison Gorge cuts through another arc of ranges before the Denison joins the Gordon.

Many of the people who have made the world aware of the value of the South-West wilderness have come to live in Tasmania from the most modified parts of the globe. Olegas Truchanas was one of the first to see more than development opportunities in the South-West. First to canoe the Denison, his name was given to the Huon pine reserve that lies just upstream of Marriotts Gorge. He was deeply involved in the fight to gain this reserve of a species and a community that have suffered a grievous reduction in area since the Hydro-Electric Commission started work in the South-West.

The Huon pine is a cypress with remarkable longevity and extraordinarily durable timber. It is most frequent by rivers and lowland lakes and like most Tasmanian pines is readily eliminated by fire. Small shrubs of Huon pine can be found along all the major rivers of the South-West, intermixed with the river tea-tree (*Leptospermum riparium*), another South-West endemic. Gnarled and twisted 'unsuitable' large trees occur in adjacent rainforest as do the stumps resulting from over a century of pining. In areas remote from river access large beds of old trees still can be found. These have not yet been recorded as attaining 5,000 years of age like the American *Pinus aristata*, but trees more than 2,000 years old are frequent.

The Gordon-below-Franklin dam would drown the Denison River up to the Hamilton Range. The Denison Gorge and Freedoms Gate would be inundated.

IN MARRIOTTS GORGE, DENISON RIVER

MARRIOTTS GORGE, DENISON RIVER

PEBBLES AND FALLEN LEAVES, MARRIOTTS GORGE

OXALIS AND FALLEN LEAVES OF CELERY TOP PINE

PEBBLES AND POTHOLE

MORNING DEW ON STICHERUS FERN

BRANCHES OF HUON PINE

Lower Gordon River

OLEGAS TRUCHANAS was the first to navigate the Gordon River when, in 1958, he made an epic voyage by canoe from Lake Pedder to Macquarie Harbour. The Gordon catchment, which lies in the 'Roaring Forties' averages more than 250 rainy days each year. Consequently, the 270-kilometre-long stream carries more water than most of the longer mainland rivers.

Less than two decades ago the Gordon's flow varied from the raging torrents of snowmelt, winter deluge and summer storm to a more dignified movement when rain and snow were gentle or absent. Now, its waters are released steadily through turbines below the arching monument to technology that traps its flow above the Serpentine junction. The large reservoir thus formed, with its ugly apron and bristle of dead trees, is fed, in part, by another reservoir which destroyed Lake Pedder in 1972.

Below the dam, the Gordon moves at intermittently decreasing pace one hundred kilometres through uninhabited rainforest and impenetrable scrub. From Macquarie Harbour to Butler Island the lower Gordon is plied by large cruisers where magnificent rain-forests are reflected perfectly in the broad, deep waters. The stark, stirring beauty of the Angel Cliffs in the limestone country upriver of the Franklin junction, is beyond the cruise vessels' reach. And the most spectacular features of all, the Gordon Splits, are hidden in the remote, rugged ranges thirty kilometres upstream of Butler Island.

Although its extremes of flow are mitigated by man, the river still runs wild and fast through the Splits, chasms excavated by water in the north-south line formed by the Nicholls and Doherty Ranges. In their narrowest parts the Splits are less than four metres wide. Their narrowness creates enormous variations in the height of the water's surface as a result of relatively minor variations in flow.

In the mid-1920's the piners Abel and Doherty explored the Splits and laid to rest years of speculation that the Gordon flowed through a vast natural tunnel.

Sticht, who accompanied Abel on a return visit to the Splits in 1928, wrote that 'Words can scarcely describe the glory of the place'. Words and pictures will be all that is left if the Gordon-below-Franklin dam is imposed on this ancient landscape.

RAPIDS IN THE SECOND SPLIT, LOWER GORDON RIVER

RAINFOREST ABOVE THE FIRST SPLIT

FIRST SPLIT FROM LOWER BASIN

FIRST SPLIT FROM LOWER BASIN

SASSAFRAS SEEDLING, FIRST SPLIT

DOWNSTREAM VIEW OF CENTRAL CORRIDOR, FIRST SPLIT

ANGEL CLIFFS, LOWER GORDON RIVER

BUTLER ISLAND, LOWER GORDON RIVER

THIS BOOK BEGAN almost twenty years ago when, as a teenager, I was introduced to rivers and canoeing by Olegas Truchanas. Over the next decade —as weekends and holidays allowed—I made many river journeys, often in the company of three or four friends. For a few days or perhaps two weeks at a time we moved in a glittering, sun-splashed world where living assumed a clarity and intensity unknown in ordinary city-bound existence. Our bodies became attuned to rock and rapid; our senses eagerly absorbed the roar of whitewater, the silent greens of the rainforest. My steadily growing skill at negotiating obstacles bolstered my self-confidence and eased the shyness of adolescence. On many of those trips Olegas was our mentor and inspiration; an artist in living who led by example and lived life to the full. He died in 1972.

The rivers we canoed were the joyful summer counterpart of skiing in winter and mountain walks in autumn and spring. The thought never occurred that one day the rivers might cease to exist, just as it seemed impossible that Lake Pedder could be obliterated. Yet one by one the rivers we had known disappeared; their forests drowned, their rushing waters trapped behind grey concrete walls. Quite suddenly, it seemed, those carefree years had come to an end. There was no place for the wild and free in the 'grand scheme' decreed by Authority. Lake Pedder, that living jewel of the wild, became part of the scheme and it too ceased to exist.

During those early canoeing years the secret world of the Franklin River remained hidden from us. It assumed an air of myth and unreality, too remote, perhaps even for the engineers who were then busily damming the more accessible streams. I listened in awe at John Hawkins' hair raising account of navigating the Franklin by heavy, two-man fibreglass canoe. Our craft, designed by Olegas, were much lighter and more manoeuvrable but the problems in negotiating the river seemed too great and I dismissed the thought of following John's example.

Years later, in 1976, two men completed the 110 kilometre journey down the Franklin without mishap or trauma. They were Bob Brown and Paul Smith. They used small rubber rafts in which three weeks' supply of food and gear could be easily stowed. The rafts handled huge rapids with ease and could be simply deflated and easily portaged around impossible drops.

And so, in the summer of 1979, and again in 1980 and 1981 I followed in Bob Brown's wake and made three full-length trips by rubber raft down the Franklin. The river was all that I had hoped and more—it was grander, wilder, more remote and touched me more deeply than any other place I had known in Tasmania's South-West. By 1980 the idea for this book had formed and I made journeys down the Denison and lower Gordon to photograph other rivers under threat from the proposed Gordon-below-Franklin dam.

These pictures, then, show a little of the wild heritage which belongs to us all and Authority says we cannot afford to keep. Yet ultimately, we will all be the poorer should the remaining wild rivers be dammed.

Peter Dombrovskis

ALL THE PHOTOGRAPHS were taken with a Linhof Master Technika on 5 x 4" Ektachrome E6 film. The book was printed in Singapore by Tien Wah Press in fine screen (200 lines per inch) lithographic process on a Heidelberg Speedmaster press. The colour separations were made with a Hell Chromograph DC350 ER electronic scanner. Paper used was Satintone Matt for the colour section and Brigadoon Scots Grey for the text section. The endpapers are Mi Tientes Canson and the book is covered in Wicotex Tamar cloth. Printing of this quality would not have been possible without the excellent co-operation and attention to detail of the staff at Tien Wah Press nor without the expert technical and artistic guidance of Rod Poole. Bob Brown's original manuscript was edited by Geraldine Brooks; any errors or omissions remain the responsibility of the publisher. The hill shading and drainage components of the map are reproduced courtesy of the Lands Department, Hobart; nomenclature is by the publisher. Photographs held by the Tasmanian Wilderness Society and in Bob Brown's private collection were used as a basis for several of Peter Jackson's drawings; the Kutikina Cave implements were loaned by the National Parks and Wildlife Service, Hobart.